Death of an Unvirtuous Woman

poems by

Suzanne Ondrus

Finishing Line Press
Georgetown, Kentucky

Death
of an
Unvirtuous Woman

Copyright © 2022 by Suzanne Ondrus
ISBN 978-1-64662-965-7 First Edition
All rights reserved under International and Pan-American Copyright Conventions. No part of this book may be reproduced in any manner whatsoever without written permission from the publisher, except in the case of brief quotations embodied in critical articles and reviews.

ACKNOWLEDGMENTS

"The Power of the Pen", an alternative version of "Silenced" published as "Wood County News, 1882" and "Tarred & Feathered by the *Wood County News*" *S/tick*: July 2019
"And the Children Sing "Mr. Carl Bach" *The Five-Two*: July 2022
"Diese Zeit" *The Five-Two*: September 2022

Publisher: Leah Huete de Maines
Editor: Christen Kincaid
Cover Art and Design: Christina Ondrus
Author Photo: Raymond DiCarlo

Order online: www.finishinglinepress.com
also available on amazon.com

Author inquiries and mail orders:
Finishing Line Press
PO Box 1626
Georgetown, Kentucky 40324
USA

Table of Contents

Abschiedskuss 1
Notice! 2
Mary's Way 3
They've All Passed   Me By 4
Let's Sell the House *Meine Liebe* 6
Termagant 8
Where's Carl? 9
Judge Cook Advises Carl: 10
The Foreman 11
And the Children Sing "Mr. Carl Bach" 12
5 Sets of Eyes on Mrs. Bach 13
The Power of the Pen 14
Driven By Their Stomachs 15
I Put Her Cruel Words Down 16
Rezept für Heimweh und Unterstützung 17
Action Tells the Story 18
Possessions Tell the Story 19
Dear Sister Mine, ... 20
Tarred & Feathered by the *Wood County News* 21
Diese Zeit 22
Carl Bach. His History and Crime Retold 24
Lightning Shift of Narrative 26
Distilled Notes 27
And the Children Sing Corn Knife: 28
Silenced 29
Evidence 31
Notes 32
Discussion Questions 34

Abschiedskuss

Scythed hay,
milked cows,

and deprived hens
echoed off the barn,

stone wall and linden tree
shoving me close

one last time

to the hear my Mother's heart
that had beat

with mine
before I was mine alone.

Abschiedskuss means a goodbye kiss

NOTICE!

REWARD
of five oil wells and continual mouths
on your dick
if brought in silent
and limp like green onions
five days old,
for the apprehension of one Mary Elizabeth Bach,
    Alias: Thunder Wolverine,
woman of sizeable stature,
wide shoulders capable
of hauling two water-filled buckets each,
unkempt,
fingernails filled with dirt,
stern blue eyes.

BEWARE,
has honey locust mouth
that looks and smells sweet,
but can shred with its thick thorns.
She is considered capable of withering
all your acres of corn with one sole stare.
If you see her, go straight to Sheriff Reid.

WANTED for pickling her husband's manhood
for all of Milton Center to see, read, and hear.

July 22, 1881

Mary's Way

He courted three weeks,
then asked for my hand.
He got them both
and my savings too.
Bought us land west
of Cleveland in Wood County.

Gone was my waiting.
Gone was my wonder.
Ahead was my plot—
my chance to get
enough for peace.
I'd staved off for riches, said

no to an orange silk bonnet,
no to crimson and gold ribbons from Paris,
no to sugar and cream in tea,
no to butter,
no to beeswax candles,
no to glycerin soap and
no to weekly letters home.

I pushed the unneeded aside—
and threw myself forward

through light-short days,
through watering eighty acres,
through hoeing in the sun
through neighbors' stares,
through unattended births,
through weeks of eating only potatoes,

so to have a solid Hof
and a *zu Hause*
for generations.

* *Hof* means "yard" and *zu Hause* means "home"

They've All Passed   Me By

                                          I'm a failed farmer,
                                          small, so small,

George is a big man
with five oil wells

who people greet with great joy,
and shout
like seeing rain
after a long drought.

Everywhere bares his mark-
the flagpole,
the church's fine copper steeple,
the redbrick school
little Lizzie's doctor's bill
and our town's Telegraph line.

Ezekiel builds the roofs
everyone wants.
He's never not in demand.
There's always a steady income
in his hand.

And Samuel who let mud
from the flood be credit!
Now greenbacks and smiles
flow in and in. Oh, is he high piled!

                                          I am small, so small.
                                          My fields barely yield
                                          for us to eat till March.

                                       I've nothing in my hand
                                       because I bought this damn
                                       bog land.
                                       And so, the best I can do is
                                       a cabin of logs
                                       cut and notched by myself.

When Herr Mueller and his milled
clapboards come by,

                                       I shut my shame tight,
                                       take a deep breath, puff up
                                       my chest,
                                       and say *nein*.

Let's Sell the House Meine Liebe

It's in the paper again—
Montana,
Texas,
Letters From Out West
to us back home in Wood County,
letters to brag to those of us tall
and wide that they there too
have gotten girth.

I can smell the air
enticing seeds to burst.
I can see the big sky
screaming opportunity and big yields.

I can feel the money
pushing up all around me
like a field of wheat ready to harvest.

If we just sell,
we can be free!
We can pay the debt.

We can buy much more
Land.
We can hire hands,
and we can reap cash.

It's in the paper again—
the stories of freedom.
Kommt, let's make a'go,

Lassen wir loss von dieses Haus!
and let's push out West,
far, far from here.

I want to invest in the future,
and become as wide as
all George's five oil wells
so I can stand proud.

*Meine Liebe means "my love"; *Kommt* means "come" and *Lassen wir loss von dieses Haus* means "let's let go of (get rid of) this house"

Termagant

Constantly making terms,
finding new ways to scold,
oh with her mouth
boy
was she bold.
Over and over
she told
and told
me what to do,
chastised me right
and left,
till there was
little of me
left.

Where's Carl?

He's in jail.
She wouldn't sign the deed,

so he struck her sound,
and then the law came in,

and he went to jail,
and he's staying there

cause he won't pay bail,
so now his crops are going

to fail. He'll be fit
to be tied when he sees that field.

Judge Cook Advises Carl:

Now I'm seeing a neighbor's quarters
as best for you,
away from all this trouble.

You can go home
to tend your crops
and livestock,
but I see no need

to go into the house
or to speak with your
wife,
just the crops
and livestock.

And I suggest
you peacefully
separate,
to each his own
in good due time.

The Foreman

Focused on his task
is how I'd describe him.
He knew he needed to get
something done, and he did it.
Through and through
he hammered and tore,
over and over till the whole roof
was done, in one day.
Tenacious.
A tenacious man is what I'd say.
He set his mind to finish
and he did.

And the Children Sing "Mr. Carl Bach"

Mr. Carl Bach, Bach, Bach
under key and lock, lock, lock
under the sheriff's eye, eye, eye
cause he slew Mrs. Bach, Bach, Bach

Just wanted to whip, whip, whip
his wife to agree, agree, agree
when not, he did the devil's deed, deed, deed.
The law he didn't heed, heed, heed.

Old Charley Dutchman, Dutchman, Dutchman
who bought wet land, wet land, wet land.
How people mocked, mocked, mocked
and so his troubles began, began, began,

till one night he flipped, flipped, flipped,
hacked Mary's head to jelly, jelly, jelly,
cut her up like a weed, weed, weed
and killed the baby in her belly, belly, belly.

Oh, the crowd's so dense, dense, dense!
Get a place at the fence, fence, fence
to see Carl up close, hang, hang, hang!
Come and pay your five cents, cents, cents!

*Inspired by the children's clapping song "Miss Mary Mack". This is meant as an audience participatory clapping song.

5 Sets of Eyes on Mrs. Bach

That woman was not a woman quite. She was harsh, gruff, with a deep voice and a bristle. Her stride was large like a stilt walker. She stood with her feet wide enough that a barrel could be between.

> God bless the children. Give them strength waiting for the verdict. The lilies of the valley are on the hill by the cemetery. Peace little ones. Our father in heaven knows you have a hard burden to bear.

I could hear her that day walking by the attorney's. It was pouring, but she was loud like an ax being ground. The window was closed. "Carl, you must pay for the children. You cannot take half."

> She got mad fast. I knew she was gonna speak when she made a fist, gathering all her points inside. Then Vati was gonna hear what he didn't wanna hear. So I went to the cows or pigs. Their sounds were like a brook calmn' me from the storm of my house.

She worked hard. Every time I came their way, she was either in the field, with the cows or pigs, with the children or in the kitchen. I never saw her just sitting with a cordial in a rocker under the tree or kneeled down reverently in prayer.

The Power of the Pen

Mary was three words:
termagant, virago, and
slatternly. The ten-inch
long corn knife delivered
her to the tar of words
slated for women. And
those words turned Mary
into pure pulp.

Driven by Their Stomachs
"Not high intelligence…only cared about bodily wants"

Driven by the stomach.
They say *fressen* in German
for when an animal eats.
That's the word I'd use
for them.
Fressers.

Devoured their plates
in two minutes.
Then they stared
at what was left
on ours.

Fressers.
Fast and furious.
Eating was serious
Had to shovel
it in.

I heard at their home
they had potatoes
twice in one meal.
Gotta make you full.

Can imagine their smiles,
after a meal of potato
dreams.

Putting Her Cruel Words Down

She squints her eyes like raisins,
and her fist thunders on the table
like a herd of buffalo.
I breathe.
But when her mouth curls, picks up speed,
and hurls,
I shove.
I swing at *You coward.*
I twist her arms at *No strength*
to eat the bitter times.
With *Go out West*
with your bad luck?
I beat on her belly.
I strike at *Coward, coward*
to tower
on top
with my wagon wheels rolling
and my staked fertile West-
ern land unfolding success-
ful after successful harvest
where I hold only gold in
my hands.

Rezept für Heimweh und Unterstützung

At the onset, when the first faint peaks appear, gather a slice of dark bread. Savor it on your tongue. If none can be had, take a teaspoon of molasses and slowly suck. Next, as the heart of the home, the hearth, becomes cool, take a ¼ teaspoon *ab und zu*. Then, when bruised face, neck, back, and hands rise to double in size, think back to your town's pub with its clanking ceramic *biersteins*. Let the flavors come together. Next, conjure up your neighbors' reaction there, how the pitchforks would parade down the street calling for *Dein Mann* and let that simmer for several hours. Now if the women folk around you just cast their eyes to the side, to the ground, comment on the weather, on each other's dresses, bonnets, or gloves, you need to then gather that stifled scream and quarter it from the top to the bottom in your own space. Melt over those strips how the women back home want to look and listen to what's inside. Crisp and crumble on top what they certainly would have asked: How and where and when? In what ways have things changed? Decorate with the *pièce de résistance*, the question they'd have asked: What planning have you done?

---

*Rezept für Heimweh und Unterstützung means recipe for homesickness and support; *ab und zu* means now and then; *biersteins* are special mugs used to drink beer out of; *Dein Mann* means your husband

Action Tells the Story

    Fleeing him.
           Through the fields.
    Under clouds.
           Breathless.
Knock.
Knock.
           In the night.

Door opens.
She tumbles
        inside.
           Soup. Touch.
Bolted oak door.
           A neighbor's house
her warm warren.
           Gasping, gasping.
Her children alone.
Ashes.   A cold hearth.
An empty side
               in the matrimonial bed.

Possessions Tell the Story

5 Pigs
1 cow
8 chickens
1 rooster: **PRIDE.**

Obedient children: **RELIEF.**

Ten sacks of potatoes
               (in the secret cellar wall):

                              SURVIVAL.

Dear Sister Mine,

Spoke with the judge while Karl was in jail.
I had to sound him out, to know what would hold.

He said when two are wanting different ways,
it is best to make two ways, and he could do that
for us in Wood County.

I just want my piece of land, my home.
The judge was the only one who looked right
at me and

I finally felt solid ground
and fresh air,
felt I could muster the strength
for the fourth child
I'd never foreseen.

At last there'll be peace!
Hope you can come after
this one's born.
I think you'll like the plains.
And maybe will stay?

Tarred & Feathered by the Wood County News

Slovenly
      like her stained dress
Virago
      like a thousand pitchforks in her mouth
Termagant
      like a tornado touching down

Slovenly,
Virago,
Termagant
            Branded
      Muddy boots,
      Ripped clothes,
Stained shirts,
Gruff tones,
      Harsh words,
      Stern eyes and
Swift pushes

      To her
      Dead
            Female
      Flesh.

Slovenly,
Virago,
Termagant

These three
Words
Boxed
Solid rules
      Against
      Female
           steps

Diese Zeit

Tucked in fright
by Father tonight.

Tucked in tight,
with *Mutti* out of sight.

Slowly, softly, we recite
a prayer to see daylight.

See, Vati was locked out despite
the cold October night,

so he broke the door with his might
and suddenly was in our sight.

Mutti in bed bolted upright.
They began to curse and fight.

She was not contrite.
Vati went out for the knife

and took it to his wife.
Up, down, left and right,

from mouth to ear he sliced,
and the back of her head he diced.

Blood jumped under the moonlight.
Blood jumped past his height.

Soon Mutti had no fight, no might.
She wasn't alright.

Her face was too white.

And she became still, so still,
like she was sleeping tight

but with her eyes forever wide affright,
and then we knew Vati had killed her *diese Zeit.*

*diese Zeit means "this time"

Carl Bach.

His History and Crime Retold

A SORROWFUL CHAPTER ACCOUNT OF THE TRIAL AND EXECUTION

On the morning of the 11th day of October, 1881 -------------------------
--------came into Bowling Green
------------------------- parcel
in his hand, staring about in a bewildered sort of way as if he might be a stranger or was looking for someone.

-----------------addressed himself to Sheriff T.C. Reid,-------------in rather broken English,--
---------------------------------"I want to go to jail."

Mr. Reid looked at him closely. His eyes, ---------------blood-shot and red, shone with an unnatural light, and betrayed great emotion and a desperate state of mind: his whole appearance denoted painful agitation.-------------
----------------------------------"Have you been having more trouble with the old woman?"

"Yes, bad trouble," said he
"Have you been whipping her again," said the Sheriff.

"Yes, I whipped her dead."

------------,
          GREAT GOD, NO!
-----------killed your wife?"
   "Yes,--------------I want to
go to jail,"------------------staring ---
-----------------, crying ----------------
   "How did you kill her, " asked Mr.
Reid----------------------
"With the corncutter,"------
"Where is she"
"In the house,"---------
"Now,"----------------
-------------"is it ---likely---
she is not hurt bad as you think."
   Here he again sobbed-------
-----incoherently said, "she is dead,
Sheriff,
          PUT ME IN JAIL

-----------he carried--------------
--------some old deed and papers-----
examining -------------------------
-----------articles from him,---------
locked him in jail--------------------
a perplexed state of mind.
   The man was Carl Bach..................
.........a German............57
years of age,............resident of this coun-
try about 22 years,-------------------------

*Found poem from *Wood County Sentinel* October 18, 1883

Lightning Shift of Narrative

When I grabbed a stick to lick,
I didn't think to kill.
You see, *meine Frau,*
made a nine-foot high fire

in me,
with her mouth:
"*Du Arschloch!* Prepare
your own
verdamnt dinner and
wash your own *geschisshen* sheets!"

When she locked me out
of my house,
she lit that pyre.
I blazed and blazed,

enraged at being shut out,
and made so *klein,*

I had to knock her
into a woman's place,
below me,
her husband,
had to shove her mouth
down to the ground
so my voice thundered

to make her realize
it was me,
her husband,
she must heed.

*meine Frau means "my wife"; *Du Arschloch* means "you asshole";
verdamnt means "damned", *geschisshen* means shitted and *klein* means
small

Distilled Notes

- Bach's letter, shows him to be a man of fair education
- The execution, was a merciful one
- The rope used, was new, made especially for the purpose
- Bach delivered all his papers up to Sheriff Brown
- He revealed his suicide tools hidden in his cell

Nearly every tree that would afford a
sight of the top of the gallows
was occupied by men and boys

>None of the Bach's children were there
>on execution day.

Bach's spiritual advisers had wonderful
power and control over him during
his last hours.

>There were probably 5000 people
>about the jail when the drop fell.

The log cabin in which the murder
was committed,---------
has burned to the ground since.

And the Children Sing Corn Knife:

Double double, this, this,
Double double, that, that,
Double this, double that,
Double double, this, that.

Double double corn corn,
Double double knife knife,
Double corn double knife,
Double double corn knife.

Double double, this, this,
Double double, that, that,
Double this, double that,
Double double, this, that.

Double double corn corn,
Double double knife knife,
Double corn double knife,
Double double corn knife.

Double double, this, this,
Double double, that, that,
Double this, double that,
Double double, this, that.

Double double corn corn,
Double double knife knife,
Double corn double knife,
Double double corn knife.

Silenced

Her throat   he grabbed, then lit
                                             for the barn. Returned, not with
                                             a stick.

There the apple tree stood.
                                             You are going to go, not me.

There little Mary with her blanket
over her eyes
wet herself.   He shoved his wife like he
                shoved
                                             a slow cow inside the barn.

Her cheek never on a pillow
more than five hours,   he sliced clear to her ear

that had caught the babies'
phlegm coughs.   He flayed her strong voice

that called dinner five times to the farthest field
                                             to a whimper. He gorged her

                    clucks:

not enough money to go to the fair this year,
not enough money for a trip to Cleveland
not enough money to buy a new wagon.
                                             and flung them on the bedroom
                                             wall,
There Katie backed against the hearth.
                                             along with a tuft of snarled
                                             hair.
                                             Slovenly.   He thrust through
                                             and through, trenched out the
the roses she never knew,
                                             the termagant and virago,
                                             varnished the walls,
                                             mirror,

                                        floor and door with her blood.

                                        Air flooded in. Filled his lungs.
                                        Quiet.

Little Carl wore   his mother's blood. Her blood
that gave four lives.

                    A willow split by lightning.

The door didn't protect her.
The Peace Warrant didn't protect her.
Her own son didn't protect her.
The fifty ears staticked in Milton Center
that had heard   Carl's crisp death threats
didn't protect her.

The smoldering,   strikes stillness,

silence, and we   remember just a moment

                  before it scavenged the ground.

Evidence

The fingers are withered, yellowed so
that it's hard to tell where the nails
are, and where the knuckles are.

For over a 100-years these fingers
have lived at the county courthouse
on public display.

They have worked beyond their years,
beyond their marrow.
From the case they holler at weeping
women who fear for their lives:

to run, take their lives and run
because that is all that matters—
not papers, deeds, money, valuables.

Take your life and run.

Notes

Death of an Unvirtuous Woman is based on a domestic homicide and domestic violence case in Wood County, Ohio in 1881. Wood County, Ohio is in northwestern Ohio. Although this killing and domestic violence took place over a hundred years ago, the cycle of violence continues today. Social, cultural, and financial pressures and rigid gender roles contribute to domestic violence. This series of poems was inspired by the artifacts of this case that in 2006 were on view in the Wood County Museum—the noose, fingers, knife, & 1883 newspaper. These relics are also chronicled in *Weird Ohio*.

The title of the book *Death of an Unvirtuous Woman* is a push back at the victim blaming of Mary Bach from 1881-1883. Three words framed Mary Bach as an unworthy woman and therefore as meriting murder by her husband. The title is so to say if women do not abide by prescribed roles, then they do not merit protection, and it is a challenge to that. My project brings in the sexist discriminatory and sensational voice in order to hold it up to the light of critique.

Carl and Mary Bach were German immigrants. Mary Bach had filed for divorce. She did not want to sell the house that she co-bought and co-owned and refused to sign the deed for Carl to sell it. In July 1881 she filed a Peace Warrant (restraining order) and weeks later filed for divorce. She was murdered October 10, 1881. She was seven months pregnant when Carl Bach murdered her with a 12-inch long, corncutter, that is a long knife used to husk corn. Carl Bach was first tried in 1882, appealed, and had a second trial in 1883. He was found guilty both times, sentenced to death, and was the last man hanged in Wood County, Ohio. He was known for saying he was going to kill Mary, and he frequently bragged about beating her up.

The 1883 newspaper *The Wood County Sentinel* victim blamed Mary Bach: "Mary had not the most angelic of dispositions. She was stubborn and head strong—a sort of termagant or virago at times, and was slothful and slatternly, almost filthy at times in her personal and house keeping habits. This came out in the testimony at the trial." Termagant, virago, and slatternly are all derogatory words solely designated for women.

Termagant (noun): an overbearing, harsh-tempered, or nagging woman

Virago (noun): a loud, domineering, violent, overbearing woman, a female warrior

Slatternly (adjective): of a woman or her appearance—dirty and untidy.

In *No Visible Bruises: What We Don't Know About Domestic Violence Can Kill Us* (2019), Rachel Louise Snyder reports that 137 women are killed every day around the world by their boyfriend, spouse or a family member (5) and that "Twenty people in the United States are assaulted *every minute* by their partners"(author's italics 6). While some men are also victims of domestic violence, women and girls make up 85% of domestic violence victims (6). Domestic violence also occurs in same sex couples.

Domestic violence is often described as a cycle, whereby there is a period of adoration, then isolation, then coercion, then abuse. This cycle repeats and it typically takes victims seven times before they leave. There are red flags:
"the quick courtship, the isolation and control, the unemployment, the medications, the narcissism and lying and stalking" (Snyder 94).

Protecting women from violence has become an international issue. The United Nations created the Convention on the Elimination of All Forms of Discrimination Against Women (CEDAW) in 1979. President Jimmy Carter signed CEDAW on July 17, 1980, but the U.S. has never ratified it. 189 countries have ratified it.

Discussion Questions

1. In "Notice!" what kind of strength does Mary have? In what parts of her body do we see her strength? What can she do with her strength?

2. In "Notice!" what is Mary's physical appearance like? How is she like a tomboy?

3. What are the two rewards in "Notice!" for a presumed man who finds Mary and what do they symbolize?

4. How might the reward for Mary's capture appeal to men in "Notice!"?

5. In "They've All Passed Me By", why does the speaker, Carl Bach, feel bad?

6. Looking at the poems "Where's Carl?", "Termagant", "I Put Her Cruel Words Down", and "Lightning Shift of Narrative" what are the excuses given to hit Mary/women?

7. The poems "Judge Cook Advises Carl:" and "Where's Carl?" point to what today we know as a restraining order. Restraining orders do not guarantee safety. Research what the consequences of breaking a restraining order in your state are. Compare those consequences to the penalty for assault. What other protective measures can a victim do?

8. In "5 Sets of Eyes on Mrs. Bach" Mary is chastised for stepping out of the prescribed role for women. How does she defy that role? What is the expected behavior of women during Mary's time?

9. Looking at "*Abschiedskus*" and "*Rezept für Heimweh und Unterstützung*", describe what Mary misses from her German culture in terms of food and German behavior.

10. List, imagine, and discuss the financial pressures in "Mary's Way", "They've All Passed Me By", "Let's Sell the House *Meine Liebe*", "Putting Her Cruel Words Down" and "Possessions Tell the Story." What financial situation are they in? What social class are they?

Acknowledgments

Appreciation for financial support from the Fulbright Foundation, Carl Duisberg Gesellschaft, and Robert Bosch Stiftung that helped shape this work.

Gratitude to Waltraut Deinert who taught me German.
Thank you to the Leopardi Writing Conference's support, and Leopardi poets: Frederick Turner, Kyrsten Bean, Alice Gibson, Rob Lynn, Cristol O'Loughlin, John Reid, Phyllis Reusche. Special thanks to Kristina Marie Darling who pushed for putting poems in different containers and expanded my vision of all that poetry could incorporate.
Susan Grimm and Literary Cleveland workshop: Andrew Field, Meredith Holmes, Cammy Sray, Deborah Rosch Eifert, Lee Chilcote, Elise Panehal, and Ali McClain.

Thank you to the Wood County Historical Society for long ago copying the original October 18, 1883 *Wood County Sentinel* Bach story for me. Thank you to Maxine Sykora of the Chagrin Falls Historical Society and Museum for directing me to historical newspapers online.

Friends who encouraged drafts: Dianne Ritchey, Narorn Seibert, Matt McBride, Elia Iafelice, Jim V. Pavlish, Penelope Pelizzon, and Sean Frederick Forbes. To Tasha Fouts for saying I could be the one to do this.

Special thanks to deceased poetry friend John Galetta, who gave much attention and support to this project, rest in peace.

Thanks for the support of my family: Christina Ondrus, John Hogan, Ray DiCarlo, and Louis Goldbach and Tom Ondrus deceased, rest in peace.

Honor and respect to my dear mother Mary Ann Leonard who endured and survived.

Suzanne Ondrus' work explores gender issues, racism, cultures, and women's sexuality. Her first book, *Passion Seeds*, won the 2013 Vernice Quebodeaux Pathways Poetry Prize for Women. She was the 2013 *Reed Magazine* Markham Poetry Prize winner, a 2017 UNESCO World Book Capital featured poet in Guinea, Conakry, and a 2018-2020 Fulbright Scholar to Burkina Faso, West Africa. She holds a Ph.D. from the University of Connecticut, an M.F.A. from Bowling Green State University (OH), and an M.A. from Binghamton University. Check out her YouTube channel Suzanne Ondrus, follow her on Twitter: SuzanneOndrus, and find updates on suzanneondrus.com.

www.ingramcontent.com/pod-product-compliance
Lightning Source LLC
LaVergne TN
LVHW041553070426
835507LV00011B/1063